NORTHERN BEE BOOKS

Scout Bottom Farm, Mytholmroyd, West Yorkshire

www.northernbeebooks.co.uk

Bumble Bees:
buzzing, beautiful, beneficial, big bees

by

Carol Ann Kearns

All rights reserved. No part of this publication may be reproduced, stored in a retrieval system, transmitted in any form or by any means electronic, mechanical, including photocopying, recording or otherwise without prior consent of the copyright holders.

ISBN: 978-1-912271-04-7

Design: SiPat.co.uk

Published by Northern Bee Books, 2017

Scout Bottom Farm
Mytholmroyd
Hebden Bridge
HX7 5JS (UK)

www.northernbeebooks.co.uk

Tel: +44 1422 882751

Bumble Bees:
buzzing, beautiful, beneficial, big bees

by
Carol Ann Kearns

For JKIII

Bumble bees are among the fuzziest, most colorful, and fascinating insects on the Earth. They are fun to watch. Their large size and bright colors make them easy to observe. They are common in gardens and meadows throughout the summer. In addition to being delightful insects, bumble bees are beneficial to humans since they pollinate many plants. Pollination allows plants to form fruits and seeds.

There are 20,000 species of bees found around the world, and of those, about 250 species are bumble bees. However, at any particular location there will not be nearly as many. You will be able to learn to recognize some of the common bumble bees in your area.

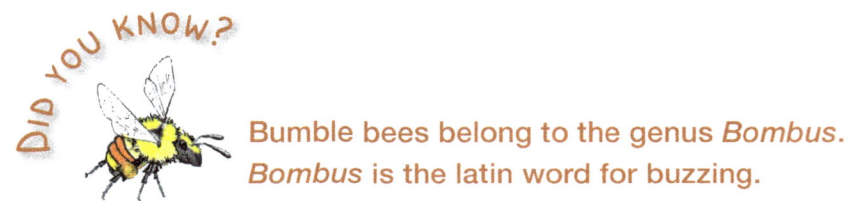

Bumble bees belong to the genus *Bombus*. *Bombus* is the latin word for buzzing.

BUMBLE BEES

Bumble bees are medium to large, hairy bees. Variations in color patterns of yellow, black, orange and white hairs help distinguish different species.

What is a Bee?

How can you recognize that an insect is a bee? Bee bodies have three main regions – a head, a thorax, and an abdomen. Large compound eyes, three small ocelli (simple, light-sensing eyes), and two antennae are located on the head. Attached to the thorax are two pairs of membranous wings and three pairs of jointed legs. Each large front wing is joined to the smaller hind wing with a row of tiny hooks that you can see under the microscope. Bees also have hairs on their bodies. Although the hairs are easy to see on bumble bees, they are not as obvious on all types of bees. Female bees have stingers, but male bees do not, meaning that male bees cannot sting. Most female bees also have a structure for carrying pollen.

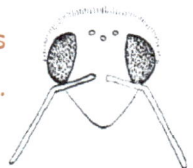

Bees have two compound eyes and three light-sensing ocelli.

BEE ANATOMY

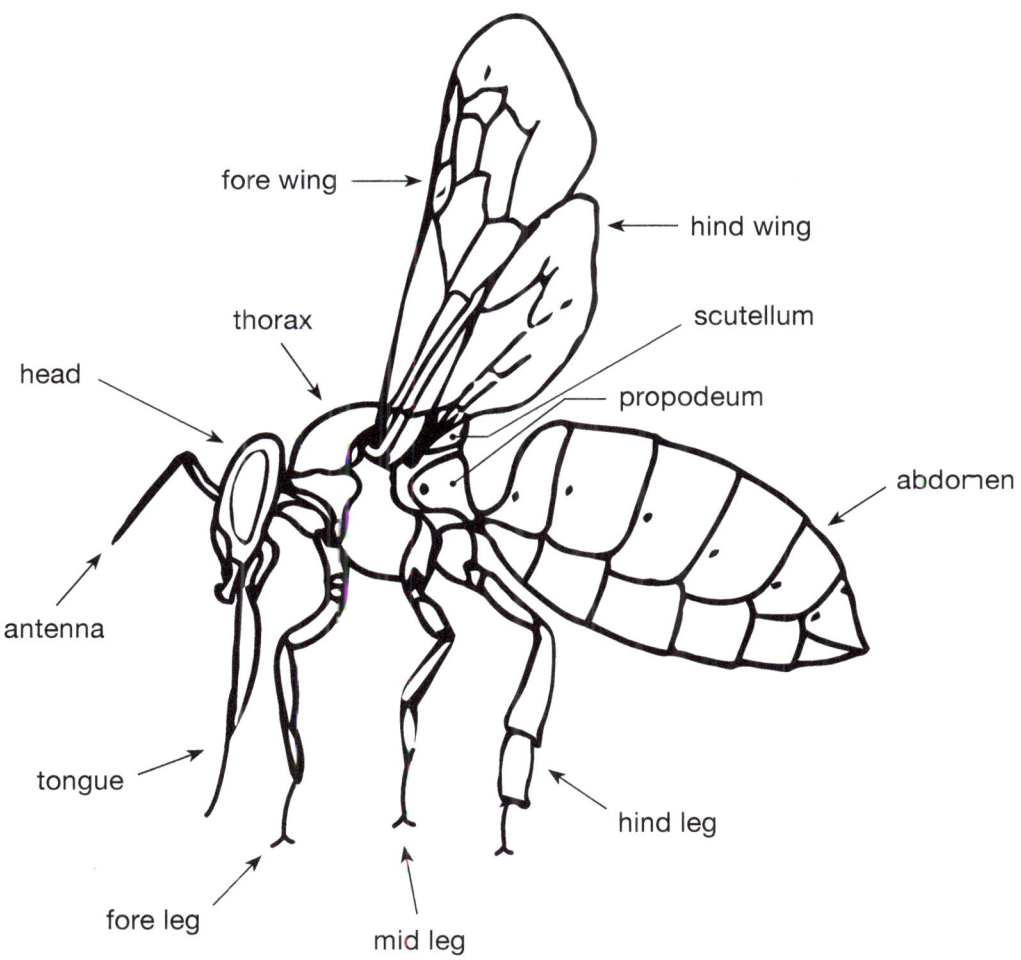

Bees have two pairs of wings. Each hind wing has a row of tiny hooks that are visible under the microscope. When flying, the hooks fit into a fold on the rear edge of the front wing, coupling the wings.

Front wing with folded edge.

Rear wing with tiny hooks.

Only female bees have stingers. The stinger is found at the tip of the abdomen.

This bumble bee carries a clump of orange pollen in a structure called a corbicula. Bees get dusted with pollen when they visit flowers, and they use their front legs to comb the pollen into the corbiculae on each hind leg.

DID YOU KNOW?

Did you know that male bees do not have stingers?

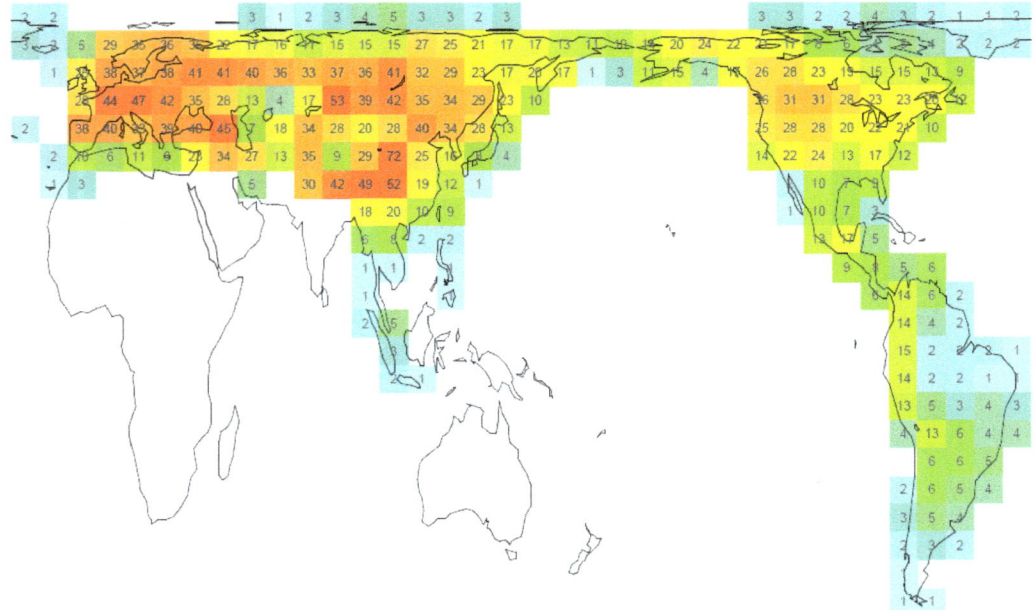

Bumble bees can be found on many continents. The numbers on the map indicate the number of species found in that part of the grid.

Most bumble bee species live in areas with cool winters, although there are a few tropical species. Unlike honey bee colonies, bumble bee colonies do not live through cold winters. Only the young queens, born in late summer or early fall, survive. Queens get through the winter by hibernating underground. A queen must mate before she hibernates so she will be ready to lay eggs in the spring. Like other animals that hibernate, young queens must eat a lot so they can live for several months without food. Once the queens have mated and stored some fat, they burrow into the soil and spend the winter underground.

Bumble Bee Life Cycle

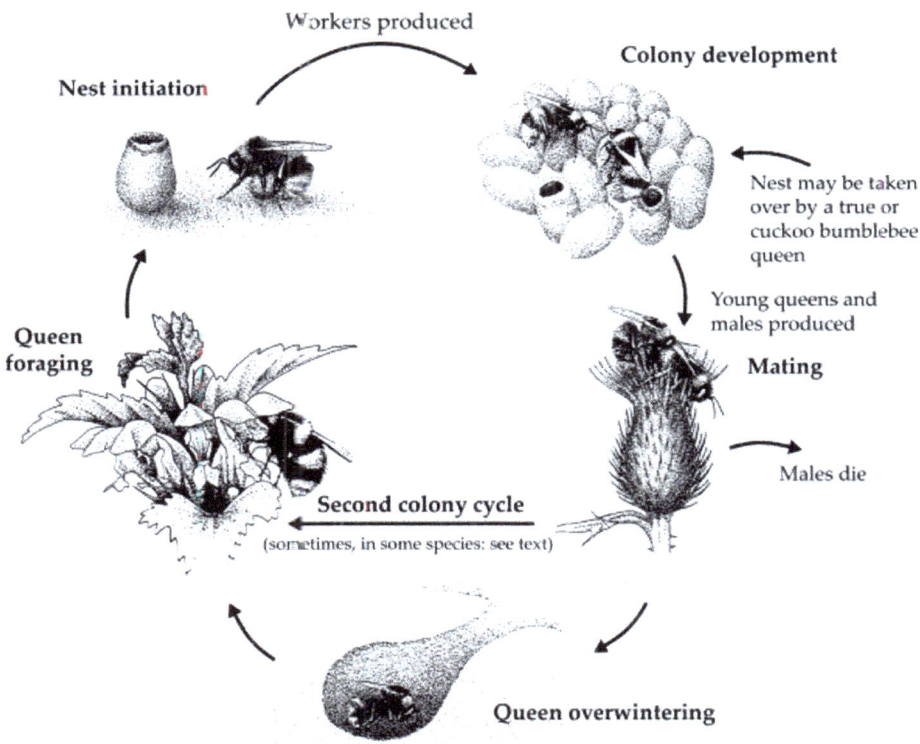

In the spring, each queen digs her way to the surface. She is hungry. She searches for flowers that hold sweet nectar she can drink. She also searches for a place to start a nest. She looks for a dry, cozy space with a small entrance that will keep larger animals out. Sometimes a queen finds an old, deserted mouse's nest, a crevice in a stone wall, or a hollow space under a log. Once she has chosen a nest, she will begin to store pollen and nectar. She makes a small cup out of wax to store nectar. The little cup is called a honeypot. The queen secretes wax from between the segments on the lower surface of the abdomen. She can shape the wax using her jaws.

When the nest is ready and there is plenty of stored food, the queen will lay eggs. The eggs hatch in three or four days. A pale larva emerges from each egg. Larvae are worm-like young bumble bees. Just as butterflies develop from caterpillars, adult bees develop from wingless larvae. Larvae eat pollen mixed with nectar. Because they cannot fly, larvae depend on adult bees to bring food to the nest.

Bumble bee larvae (above) and pupae (right). (The protective coverings have been removed so the bees are visible). Like caterpillars, bee larvae must pupate to become winged adults.

After several weeks, the larvae make cocoons, or protective coverings. Within the cocoon, they pupate – that is, they stop eating and undergo metamorphosis. The larvae change form, developing into winged, adult bees. When they first come out of the cocoon, their bodies are soft and their hair is silver. It takes about two days for them to become brightly colored. They are small compared to the queen bee. They are called worker bees because they have chores to do.

Worker bees are all females. Young workers take care of the nest, the eggs, and the larvae. They can make wax to help the queen. Some workers guard the nest entrance. When workers get a bit older, they may leave the nest to feed at flowers. They gather food for the next batch of larvae.

This is a small bumble bee nest. Note the honeypots, and the spheres that contain developing bees.

Male bumble bees have longer antennae and longer abdomens than females. Some male bumble bees have very large eyes compared to those of females.

Once there are plenty of workers to collect food, the queen bee stops visiting flowers and stays inside the nest. Now the queen's only job is to lay eggs. Worker bees take care of the new babies, their younger sisters. The colony grows. Some colonies, in cool areas with short summers, have as few as 20 bees. Other colonies may have several hundred. In contrast, honeybee colonies are much larger and may have as many as 50,000 bees.

In the late summer, the queen stops producing workers. She lays eggs that will become males and new queens instead of workers. The larvae destined to become queens get extra food and they grow to be large. Once these larvae mature into adults, the males and new queens fly from the nest and look for mates from other colonies.

Male bumble bees look different from workers. They have long bodies and long antennae due to an extra segment on the abdomen and an extra antennal segment. While queens and workers generally share the same color patterns, males may differ from females of the same species in their coloring. Males also lack stingers and lack structures for carrying pollen. After male bumble bees leave the nest, they never go home. However, males often gather in large groups at night, resting together on flowers.

Male bumble bees lack pollen-carrying corbicula so their recr legs look hairy and skinny.

How do bumble bees find mates? In some species, males have very large eyes. They wait and watch for queen bees to fly near. Some males fly from point to point along a short trail, leaving a scent at each place they stop. Queens will detect the scent. If you hold a male bumble bee (remember they have no stingers!), you can often smell their scent.

After a young queen has mated, she will fatten up and prepare for winter. She burrows 5 to 15 cm underground and remains there until spring. When winter is over and spring arrives, the cycle begins again.

Did You Know?

Did you know that the only bumble bees that live through a cold winter are queen bees? These queens start new colonies in the spring.

Pollination

Most flowers require pollination. They will not make seeds or fruits unless pollen is delivered to them. A flower can only make seeds if it receives pollen from the same type of flower. Many insects can deliver pollen. Pollinating insects include bees and butterflies, plus some flies, moths, and beetles. Some bats, birds such as hummingbirds, and even the wind can carry pollen to flowers. Bees are the most important pollinators because they not only feed themselves but constantly collect pollen to deliver to their nests. You have probably heard the expression "busy as a bee." Bees must keep busy to gather enough food for themselves and for the larvae in the nest. This is what makes them such good pollinators – they have to visit many flowers to get enough pollen for the hungry young larvae.

Bumble bees are especially good pollinators. They are very hairy compared to many other bees and pollen gets trapped among their hairs. This makes it easy for bumble bees to deliver pollen from one flower to another. Bumble bees pollinate crop plants such as beans, peas, tomatoes, blueberries, cranberries, red clover, alfalfa and more. Many types of wildflowers and garden flowers are also pollinated by bumble bees. A few examples include irises, mints, beardstongue, thistle, snapdragons, shooting stars and blanket flowers. The plants benefit because pollination results in seed and fruit production. Wildflower seeds grow into new plants that fill the meadows and forests, providing shelter and food for all animals.

Bumble bees are pollinators of many crop plants like this red runner bean.

Many types of wildflowers are pollinated by bumble bees. These bumble bees are visiting lupine, blanket flower, red clover and larkspur (clockwise from top left).

Food for People

People also depend on pollinators. Fruits and seeds feed people. Pollinators produce about one-third of all the food you eat. Imagine a world without pollinators – there would be no apples, almonds, cherries, tomatoes, or blueberries. Many of our favorite foods would disappear.

Pollinators produce at least 1/3 of the foods we eat, including most fruits and nuts.

The yellow day lily as it appears to us (left), and as it appears to bees (right). Note the dark area that directs the bee to the nectar and pollen.

This wild geranium has dark pink nectar guides that direct bees to the sweet food source.

Food for Bees

Bumble bees are not trying to be helpful by pollinating plants. They don't care if plants make seeds. They are not trying to help plants grow to provide food and shelter for other animals. They are just trying to get food from the flowers to satisfy their own needs.

Flowers that need pollinators advertise their presence through bright colors and attractive scents. Some flowers have nectar guides – spots, lines, or even bullseye patterns that direct bees toward the nectar. Bees have good color vision. They can even see ultra-violet colors that the human eye cannot

This nectar-robbing bumble bee has bitten a hole in the flower and is taking nectar. It is considered a "robber" because it takes nectar without pollinating the flower.

detect. Sometimes nectar guides are present even though we cannot see them without special tools. Bees learn to recognize and remember the colors, patterns, shapes, and scents of rewarding flowers.

Many flowers provide both pollen and nectar. Nectar is a sugar-rich liquid that provides energy for bees. Bee nectar usually contains amino acids that are also important nutrients. Pollen is the source of protein for the growing bee larvae.

Some bumble bee species have short tongues and can feed at flowers that have nectar near the surface. Bumble bee species with longer tongues can reach into flowers where the nectar is deep within a tube formed by the petals. Due to the difference in tongue lengths, different species of bees may be found on different flowers. However, sometimes short-tongued bees will bite a hole in a flower to get nectar without pollinating the flower. These bees are called nectar robbers.

This bee is carrying a load of orange lupine pollen in her corbicula. A bumble bees can carry her own weight in pollen and nectar when she flies back to the nest.

Transporting Pollen to the Nest

How do bees carry pollen back to the nest? Both queen bees and workers have large, triangular depressions located on their hind legs. These hollows, called corbiculae (singular is corbicula), are used for carrying pollen. Bees get dusted with pollen when they visit flowers. Then they use their front legs to comb the pollen from their hair. They moisten the pollen with nectar and use the front and middle legs to pack it into the corbicula. A bee can carry as many as a million pollen grains. Other types of bees may carry pollen in different structures. For example, leaf-cutter bees like *Megachile* carry pollen on a brush of hairs located on the underside of the abdomen. Other bees like *Melissodes* have very hairy hind legs for carrying pollen.

Top left: female bumble bees have a structure called a corbicula for carrying pollen. The corbicula is a large, concave, triangular surface on the hind leg.

Top right: the bumble bee is carrying orange pollen in her corbicula.

Below left: A bumble bee buzz-pollinates a tomato flower.

Some flowers are specialized for buzz-pollination. These flowers have small pores at the tips of their anthers. Anthers are the structures responsible for making and storing the pollen. The anthers of buzz-pollinated flowers must be vibrated to release the pollen. Bumble bees are one of the few types of insects that can do this. The bumble bee hangs from the flower and vibrates her muscles at a frequency that releases pollen from the small pores. The pollen showers the bee as it falls down, covering her body. She then packs the pollen into her corbiculae. Several crop plants require buzz-pollination. These include tomatoes, eggplants, potatoes, peppers, cranberries, and blueberries. Honey bees do not buzz-pollinate, so these crops depend largely on bumble bees.

TRANSPORTING PLLEN TO THE NEST

Megachilid

Different types of bees carry pollen in different structures.

Melissodes

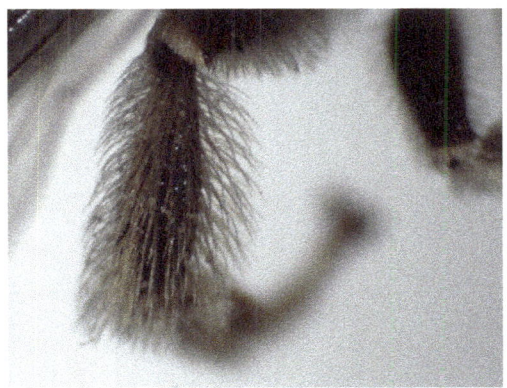

Cuckoo Bumble Bees

A female cuckoo bumble bee lays her eggs in an established bumble bee nest. She may hurt or even kill the queen so that she can rule the nest. She depends on the workers in that nest to feed and raise her young. The cuckoo never lays any eggs that develop into workers. All her eggs develop into males and females that can reproduce. The workers in the original nest are tricked into raising bees that are not their sisters and brothers.

Cuckoo bumble bee (left) takes over a nest box established by a *Bombus appositus* queen. Note the heavily armored body of the cuckoo bee. She may be stung by workers defending the nest and may have to fight with the resident queen. The fuzzier *Bombus appositus* bees on the right were the original residents.

Bee Mimics

Some flies and even some beetles look like bees. These insects cannot sting. By mimicking stinging bees, they fool predators and avoid being eaten.

This syrphid fly mimics a bumble bee. It does not have a stinger, but no predator will dare try to eat it.

Did you know? Did you know that all the worker bumble bees are females?

Which Photo Shows a Bumble Bee?

a. (top left) Leafcutter bee; leafcutter bees carry pollen on their bellies.
b. (top right) Syrphid fly – This fly mimics the appearance of a bumble bee.
c. The Bumble bee

Bumble Bee Declines

In many parts of Europe and North America, bumble bee populations are declining. Other types of pollinators, including honeybees are in trouble as well. Several things are contributing to pollinator declines. There are fewer wild places full of flowers, fewer good nesting sites, and fewer hibernation sites. Many bees suffer from parasites and diseases introduced from distant places. Insecticides and herbicides are also big problems for bees. Herbicides reduce the number of flowers available for food. Insecticides, used to kill crop pests, are often toxic to bees. Neonicotinoids, the most commonly used insecticides, are very harmful to bees. After a crop is treated with these insecticides, the chemical stays in the environment for a long time.

People who are concerned about pollinator declines can help by planting pollinator gardens. These gardens have flowers that are good sources of pollen and nectar. (For suggestions about which flowers to plant for your area, see the Xerces website (*http://www.xerces.org/pollinator-resource-center*). Bees are especially fond of native flowers. Pollinators also need natural areas for nesting. They thrive where there are wild places rather than in lawns and carefully tended yards. You can encourage schools, city parks, golf courses, power companies, and other businesses to plant some native flowers and leave wild spaces on their properties. Avoid using pesticides and herbicides. You can also get involved with organizations that support pollinator conservation, such as Xerces, the Sierra Club, and the Pollinator Partnership.

Bumble Bee Projects

You can learn more about bumble bees in your backyard, your local park or any neighborhood place that has lot of flowers. See the group activities described below.

Those who are allergic to bee stings should be observers or recorders only and should not attempt to net bees. Most bumble bees will only sting if annoyed or if their nests are disturbed. However, some bumble bee species are more aggressive than others.

Group Activity 1

Record your findings in the table below. Follow the procedure for each bumble bee that you find. Follow each bee for as long as possible.

a. With your friends or classmates, find a bumble bee visiting a flower. Give it a number or a name. One person can write in the table while two or three people follow the bee.

b. When the bee lands on a flower, notice what the flower looks like (size, color, shape). If you know the name of the flower (for example daisy or rose), write that down. If you don't, just describe the flower.

c. Watch where the bumble bee goes when it leaves the flower. Does it visit a second flower of the same type? Does it visit a different kind of flower? Remember that a flower can only make seeds if the bee delivers pollen from the same type of flower.

d. How far does the bumble bee fly between flowers? (Measure the distance, or estimate the distance by using your foot as a ruler).

e. How long can you follow the bee? How many flowers does it visit before it flies out of sight?

Bumble Bee Projects

Bumble Bee	Flower (Size, Colour, Shape)	Distance to Next Flower	Number of Flowers	Number of Types of Different Flowers Visited
EXAMPLE	1. Small Purple Bell			
Bee #1	2. Small Purple Bell	1 m		
	3. Small Purple Bell	3 m		
	4. Medium White Daisy	4 m	4	2

Record your data in the table. Then try to answer these questions.

How many of your bees visited only one kind of flower? two kinds? more than two kinds?

How many different types of flowers are in the area? Did bumble bees visit every type of flower available?

Are bumble bees good pollinators?

Do bumble bees travel very far between flowers? Why do you think that is?

What was the largest number of flowers visited by one bee before leaving the area?

Activity 2

See how many different types of bumble bees you can find. Remember that different species often have different color patterns. You can use the diagram below to color the patterns of the bees you followed. Just make copies of the diagram by using a copy machine or by tracing the outline. Then get out your crayons or colored pencils. You will need orange, bright yellow, pale yellow and black (use the white of the paper for white segments). To help you focus on color patterns, the diagram is very simple. Wings and legs are not shown.

Using a butterfly net, you can catch bumble bees and chill them*. Cold bees are inactive, and it will be easier to see the color patterns if bees are not moving. You can compare the patterns to those shown in Bumble Bees of the Eastern (or Western) United States or other on-line guides (see Additional Resources). Once you have identified two or three different color patterns, you can repeat Activity 1. Determine if different bee species prefer different types of flowers. Usually flower preference is related to tongue length, which varies among species. Bees with longer tongues can reach nectar in deeper flower tubes.

*How to Chill Bumble Bees:

- Get a small picnic cooler or insulated lunch bag. Fill it with reusable frozen ice packs.
- Catch a bumble bee in an insect net while it is visiting a flower.
- Hold the pointy end of the net up high and the bee will crawl up to the tip. Carefully work a vial or easily capped jar up into the net and capture the bee.
- Place the bee in the cooler for about 10 minutes. Check to see that it is barely moving.
- Study the bee while it is cold. Once it warms up, it will start moving and can be released without harm.

BUMBLE BEES

EXAMPLE

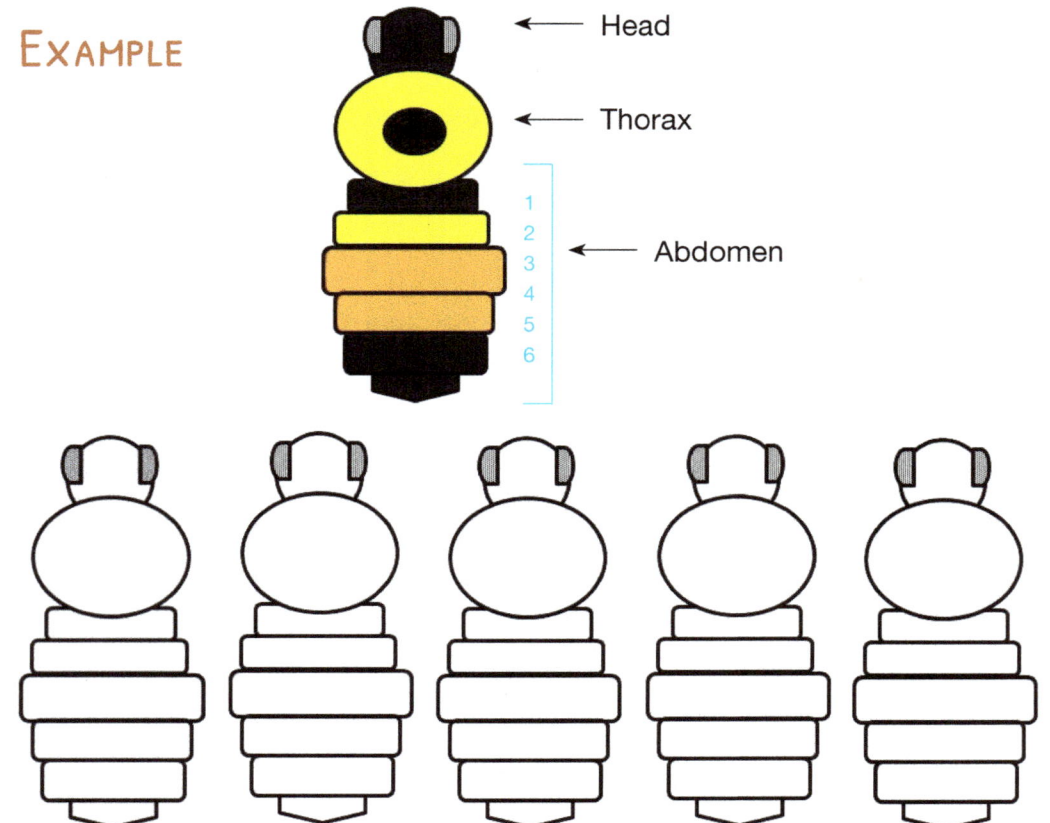

Carefully observe a bumble bee as it visits a flower. Do not move too quickly while you are near the bee or you will scare it away. Bees visiting flowers are not likely to sting unless you annoy them.

Is the head black? Does it have a patch of yellow hair?

Look at the thorax of the bee. Is it all yellow? Does it have a black dot or a stripe? Color the thorax on your picture.

Look for six stripes of color on the abdomen. While you watch the bee, call out the colors on each segment to the recorder. Color the picture so it looks like the bee. The very last segment, number 6, is quite small and has a stinger at the tip.

Try this for five or more different bees. See how many different color patterns you can find.

In most places where bumble bees occur, there are several species present. Some species can be identified by their color patterns. Look for variations in the bands of yellow, black, orange or white hairs.

Did you know that bumble bees living in high mountains and high latitudes have longer, shaggier hair than those living in warm habitats?

Additional resources

Bumblebee Conservation Trust (identification of bumblebees of the UK) https://bumblebeeconservation.org/about-bees/identification/

Bumblebee Watch (North America); Citizen Science. http://www.bumblebeewatch.org/

Colla S., L. Richardson, P. Williams 2011. Bumble Bees of the Eastern United States. USDA Forest Service and The Pollinator Partnership. http://www.xerces.org/wp-content/uploads/2008/09/Eastern_Bumble_Bee.pdf

Goulson, D. 2003. Bumblebees: Behaviour and Ecology. Oxford University Press, Oxford, UK.

Goulson D., G.C. Lye, and B. Darvill 2008. Decline and conservation of bumble bees. Annual Review Entomology 53:191–208. doi: 10.1146/annurev.ento.53.103106.093454

The Great Sunflower Project https://www.greatsunflower.org/node/1000010
Citizen Science – Help record the pollinators of your area

Kearns C.A. and J.D. Thomson 2001. The Natural History of Bumblebees: A Sourcebook for Investigations. University of Colorado Press, USA.

Koch J., J. Strange, P. Williams 2012. Bumble Bees of the Western United States. USDA Forest Service and The Pollinator Partnership. http://www.xerces.org/wp-content/uploads/2008/09/Western_BB_guide.pdf

Williams, P., R. Thorp, L. Richardson and S. Colla 2014. Bumblebees of North America. Princeton University Press, Princeton, NJ, USA.

Xerces Society. Pollinator Conservation Resource Center. http://www.xerces.org/pollinator-resource-center. Includes interactive map and regional plant recommendations for pollinator gardens.

Photo and Illustration Credits
Many thanks to the following:

Photos by Carol Ann Kearns – *Bombus* title page, wings and stinger pp. 8, 9, nests p. 13, male bumble bees pp. 14,15, bees on wildflowers p. 17, wild geranium p. 19, corbicula p. 22, scopae p. 23, cuckoo bee and nest p. 24, bumble bee p. 26 and bee cartoon.

Photos by Jeff Mitton, University of Colorado, USA – *B. appositus, B. nevadensis, B. bifarius*, p. 5

Northern Bee Books © - Bee anatomy diagram, p. 7

Photos by John Kearns, Boulder, CO USA – bee with orange pollen p. 9, bee on red runner bean p. 17, buzz pollination p. 22

Map p. 10 - reprinted from Bumblebees of North America by Williams, P. R. Thorp, L. Richardson and S. Colla 2014. Princeton University Press, USA.

Bee life cycle Illustration, p. 11 - reprinted from Naturalists' Handbooks 6: Bumblebees by Prys-Jones, O. and S. Corbet 2011. Pelagic Publishing, UK.

Photos © Dwight Kuhn, Dexter, ME USA - larvae and pupae, p. 12

Photo by Axel Ssymank, Bundesamt für Naturschutz, Bonn, Germany – Food from pollinators p. 18

Photos by Dave Kennard – day lilies p. 19, [CC BY-SA 3.0 (http://creativecommons.org/licenses/by-sa/3.0)], via Wikimedia Commons; cropped

Photo by Joaquim Alves Gaspar, Lisboa, Portugal. – nectar-robbing bee p. 20 https://commons.wikimedia.org/wiki/File:bumble bee_October_2007-2.jpg This file is licensed under the Creative Commons Attribution-Share Alike 3.0 Unported license

Photo by Michael Lamson, Boulder, CO USA – bee carrying lupine pollen p. 21, bee on lupine p. 22

Photo by Mel Harte, Berkeley, CA USA – *Megachilid* bee p. 23

Photo © Patrick 'Sarge' Murray, Lewisville, TX USA – *Melissodes* bee p. 23

Photo by David Inouye, Rocky Mountain Biological Lab, CO USA – syrphid fly pp. 25, 26, *Megachilid* bee p. 26

Watercolors by Maria Stezhko, Shutterstock

www.ingramcontent.com/pod-product-compliance
Lightning Source LLC
Chambersburg PA
CBHW061414090426

42742CB00023B/3465